The Ultimate Book of Dad Jokes That Will Sleigh You This Christmas

Shane Hannigan

What do mountains wear on Christmas?

Snow caps!

How does Mrs. Claus clean Santa's suit?

With yule-Tide!

Who brings Christmas presents to Ireland?

Saint O'Claus!

How did the carolers cross the river?

They took the Sugarplum Ferry!

Knock! Knock!
Who's there?
Frank.
Frank who?

Frankincense, Gold and Myrrh!

What Christmas carol do fish sing?

Coral of the Bells!

How are naughty elves punished?

Santa gives them the sack!

What does Santa say at the beach?

The sand is Ho-Ho-Hot!

What is Adam's favorite holiday?

Christmas Eve!

Why does Santa go down the chimney and not through the front door?

Because it soots him!

What is Santa Claus' favorite dog?

Poin-setter!

What kind of cars do elves drive?

Toy-otas!

What do elves listen to at the North Pole?

Wrap music!

What does a Christmas tree eat?

Orna-mints!

How does Frosty the Snowman stay warm and cozy during the winter?

He sleeps under a blanket of snow!

How do surfers decorate their trees?

They hang ten-sil!

Christmas is my favorite holiday!

I think I'm feeling Santa-mental!

What is every parent's favorite carol?

Silent Night!

How did the elf lose the poker game?

He had a jingle tell!

Why were the elves confused when they learned the Christmas alphabet?

Because there was Noel!

Ugly Christmas sweaters are made of what?

Fleece Navidad!

What brand of soap does Santa use?

Old Spice!

What do elves eat for breakfast on Christmas?

French mistle-toast!

Why did Santa go on a diet?

He wanted to improve his elf!

What did Mary ask Joseph when the innkeeper turned them away?

I thought you made a reservation!

Who is the most popular singer at the North Pole?

Elfis Pres(ent)ley!

How do dogs greet each other during the holidays?

Happy Howlidays!

How does a gingerbread man make up his bed?

With cookie sheets!

Why did Santa take away the elves' smartphones?

They took too many elfies!

Knock! Knock!
Who's there?
Noah.
Noah who?

Noah good cookie recipe?

What did the palm tree say to the Christmas tree?

You're looking pine!

What did the naughty soccer team get on Christmas?

COOOOOAAAAALLLLL!!!!!

What did Rudolph say when Santa gave him a book?

I already red that one!

What is baby Jesus' favorite lullaby?

Mary Had a Little Lamb!

How do the Christmas lights stay on the roof during a blizzard?

They hang in there!

Who are always on Santa's naughty list?

Fa-La-La-La-Lawmakers!

What did Santa say when he lost his boots?

I have cold mistle-toes!

Why did Donder and Blitzen get in trouble?

They were being rude-olph!

Why did the football fans cheer at the game?

Their team got a frost down!

Knock! Knock!
Who's there?
Luke.
Luke who?

Luke, in the sky, it's Santa!

Do you know why it is so cold on Christmas?

It's in Decembrrr!

How do forest animals prepare for Christmas?

They spruce it up a bit!

Why is Mom in such a good mood?

It's the most wine-derful time
of the year!

What did the parents tell their naughty children?

Yule be sorry Christmas morning!

Why was the snowman so frustrated at the hockey game?

He iced the puck!

What happens when a snowman gets mad?

He has a meltdown!

What did Santa use after he fell off a roof?

A candy cane!

Where are Christmas movies made?

Holly-wood!

What carol is played in the desert?

O Camel Ye Faithful!

How did the gingerbread man advertise his cookie business?

On Insta-graham!

How do the elves clean Santa's sleigh?

With Comet!

What kind of parties do they have at the North Pole?

Snow balls!

How does Jack Frost decline a glass of eggnog?

Snow, thank you!

Where did Santa go for a loan to fix his sleigh?

The snow bank!

What is the most popular formal dance at the North Pole?

Waltz of the Snow Flakes!

How does Santa keep track of every chimney?

He keeps a log!

Why start Christmas shopping early?

Because it is Advent-ageous!

What did Santa say when he got his new sleigh?

This has great Ho-Ho-Horsepower!

What do dogs eat for Christmas dinner in England?

Yorkie-shire pudding!

How does Santa fly his sleigh if Rudolph doesn't lead the way?

I have no i-deer!

What is the most popular Christmas cookie in Ireland?

Ginger-bread!

What song was the Christmas tree singing?

We Three Kings of Ornament Are...

What does Mrs. Claus say when she sees stormy skies?

I think it's going to rein, deer!

What did Mary ask the Little Drummer Boy?

Do you know Silent Night?

What did Santa say when he came down the chimney and saw the Cohens lighting a menorah?

Ho-Ho-Hoy vey! The Finnegans must have moved again!

What do they call Santa when he goes to the beach?

Sandy Claus!

How does Rudolph count down the days until Christmas?

On an Advent Calen-deer!

What do children do when they visit Santa at the mall?

They line up jingle file!

What is Frosty's assistant called?

His frost mate!

What did the carolers say at the Christmas tree lighting?

These decorations are
tree-mendous!

What does the Easter Bunny want for Christmas?

His two buck teeth!

What snack do the elves like to eat?

Snow cones!

When did the three ghosts visit Scrooge?

When he was Home Alone!

What martial art does Santa like most?

Karate, he has a black belt!

Knock! Knock!
Who's there?
Juan.
Juan who?

Juan to help me hang the stockings?

Which dinosaur loves Christmas?

Tree-Rex!

What did the chef say at Christmas brunch?

Tis the Seasoning!

What is the centerpiece of every Christmas table?

The letter B!

What cocktail do you serve on Christmas?

Holiday spirits!

What did one fir tree say to the other?

If I'm taking on more ornaments this year, I'll need to branch out!

What do Hawaiians drink on Christmas morning?

Mele Kaliki-mochas!

What track and field event do elves like the most?

100-yard Dasher!

Do you know the tale of Frosty the Snowman?

It's quite the ice capade!

How did Joseph make Mary coffee on Christmas?

Hebrew-ed it!

Do you know why it's so hard to find Advent calendars?

Because their days are numbered!

What carol do farm animals sing?

It Came Upon a Midnight Steer!

Why did the Christmas tree go to the barber?

He was due for a trimming!

This is going to be the best
Christmas ever!

Fir sure!

What did the elves cheer at
the stakes race?

Run, Run Rudolph!

What did the audience do at the end of the Nutcracker?

They gave a round of
Sant-applause!

How does Santa deliver presents to fish?

He drops them a line!

How do reindeer decorate their homes?

With hornaments!

What is the most popular fruit in France at Christmas?

Pear Noel!

What carol do vegans sing?

Soy to the World!

What did the mechanic charge Santa Claus to repair his sleigh?

Nothing, it was on the house!

Where are the Martinis staying for Christmas?

At the Holiday Gin!

How do Italians travel to visit family on Christmas?

On the Polar Espresso!

What is every bartender's favorite carol?

Brew Christmas!

Does Christmas ever come before Thanksgiving?

Only in the dictionary!

How did people used to talk on the phone during the holiday season?

They used an Auld Land Line!

Where does Santa keep his suit during the year?

The claus-et!

What is your wife's favorite Christmas film?

It's a Wine-derful Life!

If Santa taught high school what would he teach?

Chemis-tree!

Does Santa carry money with him?

No, he is nickel-less!

Knock! Knock!
Who's there?
Sawyer.
Sawyer who?

Sawyer family at midnight mass!

What do snowmen eat for breakfast?

Frosted Flakes!

How did the cat greet the dog on Christmas?

Have a Meowy Christmas!

What did the Advent wreath say to the candles?

This Christmas is lit!

What kind of bears live at the North Pole?

Polar Brrrrrs!

How do you access Santa's Naughty and Nice List on his computer?

Yule log-in!

How do elves pay for their toy making supplies?

With jingle bills!

What did the latte say on Christmas morning?

What a brew-tiful holiday!

What Christmas dessert do palm trees like most?

Cocoa-nuts!

Do you know why Jack Frost is so relaxed?

He's pretty chill!

What was the reaction of
the three kings when
they saw
baby Jesus?

They were star struck!

What speech did the CEO give at the office holiday party?

A mistle-toast!

How do farmers prepare for Christmas?

They Ho-Ho-Hoe the land!

How does Christmas end after the festivities?

With the letter S!

What's the best wine for the holidays?

Pinot More!

Where do math professors go to celebrate on New Year's Eve?

Times Square!

What is Mary's donkey's favorite book?

Don Key-xote!

What did the stamp say to the Christmas card?

Stick with me and we'll go far!

Where does Santa swim for exercise?

The North Pool!

Why is Frosty the Snowman so forgetful?

He's a bit of a flake!

Why do snowmen crack jokes when they first meet you?

They want to break the ice!

What did Mrs. Claus say to Mr. Claus at dinner?

Please, have some myrrh!

What happens when an elf eats too many candy canes?

He gets Tinsillitis!

What does Santa eat Christmas morning?

Brrrr-eakfast!

Why did the lobsters get coal in their stockings?

They were shellfish all year!

Knock! Knock!
Who's there?
Hugo.
Hugo who?

Hugo-ing caroling tonight?

Why does Santa take his coffee without milk?

He prefers a non-deery creamer!

Why was the Christmas tree whispering?

The holly was leaves dropping!

What kind of cookies do elves eat?

Shortbread!

What Christmas drink do teachers like?

Hot chalk-olate!

What did the explorer
say when he spotted
the island on
Christmas Day?

Fa-La-La-La-Land Ho!

What flavor of gum do Christmas trees like?

Winter Green!

What carol do animals sing in the Rainforest?

Jungle Bell Rock!

How does Jack Frost get around?

By icicle!

What holiday treat do dogs eat?

Peppermint bark!

Knock! Knock!
Who's there?
Easton.
Easton who?

Easton, west, north and south.
Santa goes everywhere!

What fast food do snowmen eat?

Icebergers!

How do they serve drinks at the North Pole?

On ice!

Why did the gingerbread house fall down?

Its foundation was crumby!

Why does the Grinch hate "knock-knock" jokes?

Because there's always Whos there!

What did the Atlantic Ocean say to Santa as he flew over on Christmas Eve?

Nothing, it just waved!

How can you tell when Santa is in your house?

You can sense his presents!

What does a Christmas tree wear when it's cold?

A fir coat!

What weekday is every child's favorite in winter?

Snow Day!

What did the train conductor say to his wife?

Baby, It's Coal-ed Outside!

What song does a snow globe sing?

"Shake Me Up, For it to Snow-Snow"

("Wake Me Up, Before You Go-Go" ~ Wham)

25 Days until Christmas!

This is claus for celebration!

Why were the church bells tired after Christmas?

They were put through the ringer!

What did Santa say when the elves fell behind schedule?

This is snow laughing matter!

What did the snowflake say to the ground?

We should stick together!

What did the abominable snowman give to Santa for Christmas?

A YETI for his hot cocoa!

How do the elves travel around the North Pole?

The Polar Express.

What did the champagne bottle say on New Year's Eve?

Pop!

How did Scrooge score the winning goal?

The Ghost of Christmas passed!

Do you know why Christmas trees can't sew?

They always drop their needles!

Why did the shepherds visit baby Jesus in the manger?

They herd the Angel's message!

How did Rudolph do in school this year?

He aced his reindeer games, but went down in history!

What is a Nutcracker's favorite dessert?

Chocolate Mousse King

What Christmas carol does a shark sing?

"Santa Jaws is Chumming to Town"

Can you believe Christmas is tomorrow?

I am snow excited!

What do monkeys leave out for Santa on Christmas Eve?

Milk and chocolate chimp cookies!

Besides toys, what else do elves make?

Radio jingles!

Which cartoon character is Santa's favorite?

Chimney Cricket!

Where do snowmen check for the weather reports?

On the Winter-net!

What does Santa eat for breakfast?

Jolly donuts!

What words of encouragement does Santa tell the elves as December 24th nears?

You can(dy) cane do it!

What did the baker sing on Christmas?

We whisk you a Merry Christmas!

What did Santa say when he almost fell off a roof?

Whoa, that was a claus one!

How does the candy cane maker reward his workers?

Higher pay-mints!

What do you call Santa if he lands on a lit fireplace?

Crisp Kringle!

What did the skier say to his wife before he jumped off the ski lift?

Alpine for you always!

What did the mother say to her crying child at the mall?

There's no need to claus a scene!

Why do the elves love the movie Diehard?

It stars Spruce Willis!

What kind of cake do they serve at the North Pole?

The kind with lots of icing!

What game do the reindeer like to play?

Truth or Deer!

How does a gingerbread man prepare for the holidays?

By **stocking** up on his favorite treats!

What does McDonald's serve on Christmas?

Bah humburgers!

What music do Mr. and Mrs. Claus listen to?

Instru(mint)al!

If you're naughty, you get coal in your stocking!

Simple claus and effect!

Why did the snowman marry the snow woman?

It was love at frost sight!

What was the turkey singing all day on Christmas?

"Simply Having a Wonderful Christmas Thyme"

What was Adam's first question?

What are you doing New Year's, Eve?

What did Tiny Tim want for Christmas?

Nothing, he's cute as the Dickens!

Why does Santa like comedians?

Because they are Ho-Ho-Holarious!

What's a penguin's favorite carol?

There's Snow Place Like Home for the Holidays!

What happens when you put gifts under a Christmas tree?

It lights up!

How do elves learn in kindergarten?

By snow and tell!

Why are candy canes so popular?

They bring merri-mint!

Who is never hungry on Christmas?

The turkey, it's always stuffed!

What did Santa Claus say when he heard Nat King Cole's "The Christmas Song"?

Oh, this old chestnut!

What did the toy salesman say to his customers?

But wait, there's myrrh!

What is the first subject that elves learn in school?

The elf-abet!

What did Santa say after he inspected his workshop?

Everything is in (pepper)mint condition!

What did the puppy say after he opened his presents?

This Christmas is pawfect!

What perfume does Grandma wear on Christmas?

Mother Ginger's Poli-Chanel No. 5!

Where do young Christmas trees go to learn?

Elementree school!

How does a penguin build his home?

Igloos it together!

Do you know how to get a really good price on a sled?

You have toboggan!

How can you tell if a Christmas tree is a dogwood?

By its bark!

Knock! Knock!
Who's there?
Mary.
Mary who?

Merry Christmas everyone
and Happy New Year!

Printed in Great Britain
by Amazon

15217245R00072